EVERYTHING WAITS TO
BE NOTICED

OTHER BOOKS BY CAROL A. ARMSTRONG

Gifts and Bequests (1996)

Patchwork of Days (1992)

Thoughts for Your Penny (1992)

Legible on Snow (1982)

EVERYTHING WAITS TO BE NOTICED

Poems by

Carol A. Armstrong

Antrim House
Simsbury, Connecticut

Library of Congress Control Number: 2011940119

ISBN: 978-1-936482-11-5

Printed & bound by United Graphics, Inc.

First Edition, 2011

Cover Art by Cary A. Rothe

Photograph of the author by Cary A. Rothe

Book Design by Rennie McQuilkin

Antrim House
860.217.0023
AntrimHouse@comcast.net
www.AntrimHouseBooks.com
21 Goodrich Road, Simsbury, CT 06070

For Jim
the other half of my thought,
my laughter, and my life —

Animae dimidium meae.

ACKNOWLEDGEMENTS

The following publications first issued poems contained in this volume, some in earlier forms:

Still Puddle Poets: "How Do You Know It's a Poem?" "The Recently Dead," "Reluctant Names," "Tree Lesson"

Still Puddle Poems—More Poems: "Topography," "The New Face of Old Age," "When the Time is Right," "Once on a Time"

Thoughts For Your Penny: the poems which appear in this volume under the title, "Things Noticed," as well as those on pages 18, 23, 34, 56, 57

I am greatly indebted to poet and friend, Phyllis Beck Katz, who lent her wise counsel, attentiveness, informed judgment, and a generosity of time to the reading of this manuscript.

To Elizabeth Armstrong, whose sensitivities, acute perceptions, and honest responses I trust and value highly, and whose skill with the computer has contributed immeasurably to bringing this book into being, my special gratitude.

To James I. Armstrong, Jr., for his ear exquisitely tuned to the music of poetry, its words as well as its silences, what it says as well as what it doesn't say, my abundant thanks.

For her elegant and seeing eye, and her capacity to make something beautiful out of the materials at hand, I am grateful beyond telling, to my daughter, Cary Armstrong Rothe, for the cover art gracing this book, which she titled "Tanks—Abstract."

And to Rennie McQuilkin, my gratitude for his skilled editing, his good eye for layout and design, and his gentle suggestions, which have guided this book into print in its present form.

TABLE OF CONTENTS

PRELUDE

I

II

III

FINALE

Twenty-eight geese in sudden flight
The last star on the edge of the night
A single button come undone
The middle child, the prodigal son
Everything waits to be noticed
A trickle underneath a dam
The missing line from the telegram
Everything waits to be noticed

from "Everything Waits to be Noticed,"
Art Garfunkel, Buddy Mondlock, Maia Sharp

EVERYTHING WAITS TO
BE NOTICED

PRELUDE

I Shall Make Poems

I shall make poems
long after I've forgotten
my middle name,
what cinnamon is for
or why the unfamiliar place
I sleep is not the home
of my childhood.

The words will seem at first
enigmatic and oracular, then
untranslatable, unintelligible.
They will abandon agreed-upon usage,
assume an unruly logic —
but the rhythms will remain
to carry the burden of meaning.

Listen for the tumbling syllables
of my laughter, the slow spondees
of my satisfactions.
Listen for dactyls waltzing
my amazements in spiraling circles,
for the joyful anapests
galloping wildly like children
knee-deep in new snow.

The words will become
the music — pure music,
embedded deeper than

the deepest reservoirs
of memory gone dry.

Then speak wholly nonsense to me —
sing back to me, transposed,
the answers to my love letters.

Not for Monday

On Good Friday morning
a poem came to my sister
even before she was dressed.
She wrote hurriedly on
fourteen pieces of toilet paper.
It was a song of praise.

On this same morning
I went looking for a poem.
I needed one for Monday.
Poems do not come for Monday.

They come for first-light noticing,
for resonating taut-tuned gut.
They come to order a disarray of words
tossing, restless on a bed of anticipation.

They come open-faced
as a child to wonder,
trusting as a babe
to the arms of exaltation.
They come bringing with them
the language of their mysterious origin.

They come, wary wild things,
ready to turn tail at the first
sign of coercion...and they
never come for Monday.

How Do You Know It's a Poem?

If it tastes tart and sweet on the tongue,
if it whispers and thunders by turns,
if it builds vast sunsets out of small, tinted words,

if it sounds like the ocean dragged by the moon
   over the corrugated mountains of the sea-bottom,
if it catches you in the rocking of the body's wild forgetting,
   the heart's inconsolable remembering,

if it compels your attention by
   turning the expected upside down
   as the landscape reflected in the glass-smooth lake
   brings treetops to the tips of your boots,

if the shards of a grief are gathered into its
   kaleidoscope of mirrors, multiplying it
   to a shapely meaning,

if a boisterous joy fills its sail
   surfing you to shore, breathless and laughing,
if it sets you on edge with a sharp discontent,
   reminds you of things you never knew,

if it provides a vademecum, a map, a *carnet de passage*
   to the true country of paradox
   haunted by the spirits of things past,
   yet to come, never to be,

if it mimics a piñata eagerly waiting
   to release its messages, while you
   beat about it blindfolded, searching,

if it whistles a lilting tune which
   will not leave your head,
   walks beside you humming till
   you must move in its rhythm,

if it tosses sea-smoothed pebbles into
   a bowl of tears till they spill over,

if it picks the lock of your keep,
   entering past the blindered eyes
   of your zealous guard,

if it cuts through a thicket of thorns
   to wake you from the sleep of a hundred years,

chances are — it's a poem.

I

Once on a Time

Once on a time when the world
was new and I was new
things presented themselves to me

one at a time to be named
as did the animals to Adam
in the first creation.

And I gave them names
made from the syllables
I found in my mouth and

the naming gave me pleasure.
Each thing then belonged to me
and I was satisfied.

Later the world became old
even as I, and it was full
of distinctions, categories

divisions, and my mouth
was filled with names
not of my own choosing

and the syllables had to be reshaped
to speak even the simplest truths
or the most transparent philosophies.

Is there not some dispensation of grace
by which one may come again to that
language of unencumbered newness

delicious in the mouth,
satisfying the heart's hunger
for the gladness of Eden?

The Curve of Time

The mock orange in the summers
of my twenties bloomed extravagantly
for months in felt memory.

In the summers of my nineties
the tight white buds cupped in green
seem to unfurl on Thursday and
by Friday shed a snow-shower of
petals in the June breeze.

Blueberries, when I was young
carpeted the fields. Harvesting them
occupied an eternity — at first,
of excitement then of hot midday
tedium with tag-along child eating
his way through the low-bush.

Now, from ripe to rot happens
while I'm still looking for the painted
berry bucket with the string to sling
around my neck, preventing spills
while bending over to pick.

Scientists play with Time and its
idiosyncrasies as with an intricate toy
using its plastic properties

to bend it, twist it, tie the frayed ends
of it in their knotted logic — all quite
unsuitable for use in my pocket-watch world.

But are they onto something,
these playful minds, explorers of the Relative?

$$\frac{ripe\ blueberries}{90} \times noon + 78° = slower\ I\ /\ faster\ time - \pi$$

When I Was Young

When I was young the world was flat
except for mountains, hills, and things like that,
and everybody had three healthy meals a day
except, of course, Armenians who starved
a half a world away.

The sun came up each morning bringing light.
I never thought to wonder where it spent the night.
The moon in divers shapes lit up the dark,
but could not drive the scary shadows
from the nearby park.

All puppies, lions, horseshoe crabs, the sea
were put on earth especially, I thought, for me.
The only tragedies I had to face
were pea soup, whooping cough, and moving
to another place.

Since then I've learned the earth is really round
and gravity's what keeps us on the spinning ground.
The moon revolves around the earth, and both, the sun,
and even one square meal is not
assured for everyone.

The world has changed, or my perception of it
which does not mean I don't still fiercely love it.

Only Once

I thought it would be there
always
because I saw it once.

I thought I could look
another day
and all would be the same.

The Madam

It was not usual to see
my father raking leaves
so when I saw him
in awkward stance
rake in hand on our
cliff-steep front lawn
among the mountain laurel
blossoms long gone
the sycamore's huge leaves
blanketing the slope,
my child-eyes
noticed everything:

his Saturday raggedy sweater
his artist's hands holding
the rake handle delicately balanced
more like an out-sized paint brush
than a garden tool,
with his attention not on
the crisp, shushing leaves
slowly being tumbled
toward the stone wall.

I noticed the damp earthy
fall smell, the late-day lights
coming on in the gabled

house across the road
which had been recently rented
to a lady we didn't know
who kept strange hours,
had a succession of visitors
at odd times of day and night
their cars parked up the road
or down the road —
never by the house.
I, as a child given to inventing
reasons for unexplainable things
decided there must be
an invalid in the family with
an illness of the eyes, for
the shades in the house,
where before I had been
accustomed to play,
remained drawn most of the day
in the sun-struck windows.

I sensed an aura of importance,
of solemn role-playing
in the scene, carved into
my childhood memory
like initials in a schoolhouse desk.

When the police arrived
later that night, long after
I was innocently in bed,

to raid the thriving business
which had sprung up in an
unaccustomed neighborhood,
Mother, ever the hospitable hostess,
was at a loss as to what to serve
the constabulary who were
stationed in our front room.

I was told my father's answer
to her social dilemma was,
"Horehound Drops, my dear!"
I failed to see why policemen
who didn't have coughs
needed cough drops, though
they did taste rather good
when Granny slipped us one
during a particularly long sermon.

A Fine Fair Thing

It is a fine fair thing
to have someone
wave to you with
upraised arm
as he rides a great
orange tractor
in from the fields.

It's a thing to be treasured
to have someone
poach an egg & fry a tomato
from his garden for you
and sit contented across
the breakfast table
thoughtfully sipping coffee.

'Tis a wonder to have someone
to fight with when
you've a need to fight
and know in your bones
with a certainty beyond reason
that he won't leave you
forever, alone with your anger.

Paradox

When I am with you
I cannot sing.

When I'm away from you
it's you who
makes me sing.

Uses of Old Argument

We're lost once more
in the miasmic fog
hanging over the bog
of our disagreement.

Always the same igniting spark.
It's an old argument
nickel-plated to mimic
the importance of silver

always in the same vein,
an old argument
completely scripted
lines repeated so often

they come *sans* prompting
as expected cue's delivered,
scene blocked out, Saturday matinee
Thursday evening the same,

no need to listen, to adapt,
to invent a new outcome
improvise an alternative ending.
Blind to persuasion, like moles

we tunnel in subterranean dark
toward imagined certainties
leaving unanswered questions
at point of entry, in a pillow of dirt.

We are no longer clever
or inventive. We lost interest
years ago but we play it out,
this old argument, which serves

to assure ourselves and each other
that we are indeed *separate and equal*.

Priestess of Vesta

I am dedicated for life to the sacred
task of keeping the saltcellars filled
seeing the laundry's folded
and light bulbs replaced.

I am the one responsible
for mittens and manners
birdfeeders and broccoli
clean underwear and good grammar.

Dispenser of questionable answers
and unquestionable truths
I am the transmitter
of nursery songs and fairy tales.

It is for me to please and appease
the gods of Mood and Madness
providing the laughter needful to survival
and keeping the spirits' woodstove stoked.

I am the intercessory presence
between those under my roof
and the capricious demi-gods
of Untidiness, Chance and Cruel Joke.

My daily rituals include
sweeping up the dirt from
garden boots and sand brought in
by beach-brown children.

I am honored as Vestal
chosen long before
there was a chance for choice
with the priestly formula

Te, Amata, capio.

Robert Lowell Remembered

The night I entertained Robert Lowell
my husband was away from home.

At dinner he imagined the Chair
of the English Department to be my husband

and was mildly surprised when he left
with another woman.

When the other guests had departed,
my small daughter in bed

he patted the sofa beside him, saying,
"Come sit here by me."

I countered that the light was better
where I sat embroidering initials

on a double damask dinner napkin,
a little shy of his "reputation."

His rather too complete biography
had appeared recently in *The New Yorker*.

I remember asking if that had altered
the way he was able to move among people.

I think he said No, but I was not sure
I believed him, nor he, himself.

He asked for hot milk before bed.
I brought it on a silver tray

with a decanter of sherry and
a shaker of nutmeg.

Leaning over the bannister
he kissed me goodnight.

He left his watch among
the rumpled bed-sheets. I sent it on.

I have his autograph somewhere among
my memorabilia, for he wrote me

a 5 cent post card of scrawled
well-brought-up thanks.

What Do Crows Think?

What do crows think of snow?
What is the moon to them —
or Tuesday or pearls?
And what of the machines
that lay out feasts for them
on the ribbon of speeding highway?

In their black robes do they
pass judgement and announce
the verdict from their high perches?
Am I judged a slattern
when I escape my summer kitchen
leaving my woodstove
to do the work of baking?

Am I noticed as I stretch out
on the side stoop in the sun,
the smell of earthy things
contenting my spirit,
shreds of a new poem
fluttering lazily in my head?

How may I plead my case?
Can my judges be swayed
by black oil sunflower seed?

Autumn

On my front stoop the pumpkin
at first frost is collapsing into itself.
The joints of my old chairs are coming unglued.

The order of my files has become haphazard
as have the layers of my remembering.
Things I need find me, not I them, if I'm lucky.

The young white birch has spent all but
a few of its gold coins, which cling still
to the random tracery of bare twigs.

There's a first tentative dusting of snow
on the last furled rosebud, still expectant
and in my old heart a song struggles

to free itself from the entanglements of a sorrow.

Reluctant Names

Familiar names no longer come with speed at need.
They linger in the anteroom of consciousness,
to my distress. They line up in a ragged row,
their pace so slow

it's difficult to know just when they will appear.
They show up, yes, they show, but several hours hence,
no longer apropos. They come and go at will,
not mine but theirs.

And sometimes in the middle of a sleepless night
the selfless Florence Nightingale will wander in
upon a whim, and wander off again to ease
some soldier's pain.

King Polybus comes next, the father of the hexed
King Oedipus, not him he slew — the one he knew
as father in his youth, before the truth came out
and horror reigned.

Then Pan...and Anne of Cleves, who leaves when she discovers
she's become irrelevant, and after Anne
comes our new plumber's son, the one whose name's the same
as Father's nurse,

and she hangs back for lack of relevance. Her stance
is hesitant and shy, and wondering why she's called,
retreats. This scene repeats itself throughout the day
and into night

as well-known names continue to refuse the clues
I use as bait. I wait, and play these foolish games
to bring to mind, through memory's portcullised gate,
reluctant names.

Mirrored

In a sudden mirror
the startled sight of me
reflecting
the gray outside only

nothing of the child-colors
marbling the inside.

Beyond the Reach of Words

With the man of precise logic
and intellectual acuity
who honors language and trusts
the sturdy meaning of words —
you can dissemble.

With the man whose logical links
have fallen into disrepair,
whose mind has become wayward,
insistent on its own tattered reality,

whose words have wandered off
into a dark forgetting
while crows feast on crumbs
scattered to show the way back —
you cannot dissemble.

He is quick to discern disaster,
is quieted by your quietness.
You cannot mask irritation
or feign contentment. He lives
in your interior weather, is
beyond the reach of argument.

Words are blunt instruments unequal
to the delicate task of dissembling.

Usefulness

I

Mown hay lies *making*
in the August sun.
Does it look wistfully back
at greening and growing?
Does it know its usefulness
is still to come?

II

The young spruce
proud of its branching
looking to become
choir loft for birdsong
is cut down in December.

In its bewilderment
can it envision the glory to come
when it's hung with lights
reflected in ornaments
glistening with memory

and in the wide eyes
of children seeing it
for the first time?

III

And what shall we say of
the old poet with the gentle smile
who speaks essential truths
in careless chronology
substituting silence
for unbidable words?

Does he know,
being who he is
is more important
than the exact manner
of his speaking?

A Coming Together

I

The Great Blue Heron,
legs trailing at an easy angle
anticipating a landing
at our small farm-pond

flaps its wings with
unhurried grace,
its shadow scurrying

across the stubbled field
to meet it at the smooth
dark water's edge.

II

My voice sings back to me
across the echoing lake.

If my timing is right I could
be in harmony with myself.

III

Already — incised
on the polished surface
of a single stone,
our names and birth dates,

absurdly — as sure
of our marriage
as of our death.

Emily Rose

"Grandmother," said Emily Rose,
"Will you take everything
from this house to your new house
when you move?"

"Yes, Em, I shall."
"Even the cookies?"
"Yes, Em, even the cookies."

"But, Grandmother, what
will you do with the memories?"

Little Emily Rose, you
will come to know that
memories are portable.

Like the *lares* and *penates*
of Roman times, they are
carried to the new hearth,

the *penates* being the gods
of the family larder
(overseers of cookies, Em)

while the *lares* are the spirits
of the loved dead who will
go with you, laugh with you,

comfort you, tousle your head
in loving gesture, walk
by your side whispering

and being present to you
wherever you go, bringing
with you your household gods.

That's what your Grandmother
will do with the memories, Emily Rose.

II

At the Time of Greatest Darkness

At the time of greatest darkness
there is the greatest felt need
for celebration,

for the flickering illumination
of candles reaching into the world's
dark places,

for the ordinary, homely miracles that
stand against disaster, destruction
and despair,

for the small, sturdy symbols
of inextinguishable hope that
encourage us

not to mistrust the strength
of the gentle, the decent,
the comic, the kind,

for ritual words that give shape
to shared memory, carrying with them
believable promise,

for laughter that snuffs out fear,
and for an irrepressible merriment
obliterating darkness.

Gift Catalogue

Nestled in a cradle of
juniper and cranberry,
dusty-blue berries
and red ones,

a pear half,
white sweet flesh
dripping with juice,
so perfect,

so evocative of the best
of old memories,
so right and proper as
a gift for my sister

who shared ripe pears
with me on the same
sun-warmed rock in the
same childhood.

Gifts and Bequests

on the occasion of the welcoming of a new child

I give you
> rain, the puddle and rainbow maker,
> the thirst quencher,
> the mother of snow.

I give you
> the sunset song of sky
> echoed on the evening lake,
> the syncopated water-music
> of the rock-tumbled brook,
> the yearning downdrift of a modulation,
> the dawn song of the first-stirring bird,
> the huge glad sound of father-laughter
> and mother-singing.

I give you
> the beguiling shapes of Jack-in-the-Pulpit
> and Lady's Slipper
> and the secret places they grow,
> the mottled cows' slow grazing
> and windrows of August hay.

I give you
> the quick chipmunk, the slow turtle,
> the preposterous presence of
> puffin, pelican, and penguin,
> delirious dolphin-play
> and the songs and satisfactions
> of great gray whales.

I give you
    ships and steam shovels
    cogs and wheels, ratchets and cams
    levers and fulcrums
    by which, given a place to stand,
    you can move the world.
    Archimedes said so.

I give you
    things about which to be curious:
    mirrors and magnets, cockroaches' biological clocks,
    the tunnelings of the mind, the drift of continents,
    the usages of words and the creative imaginings of genius.

Of course, I give you
    the still-mysterious moon
    and showers of far stars,
    fair nights of hushed winds
    and hard nights split by lightning-storm.

And I wish you
    the taste of another language on your tongue,
    of sushi, pizza, and curry,
    of a hundred ways to say "thank you"
    and "I'm sorry."

I also leave you
    rocky hills to climb
    and injustices to battle,
    blues to sing
    and wild catastrophes to bear,
    disadvantages to overcome

and worthy things to attempt,
risks to take,
anger to tame and prejudice to pry loose.

And I wish for you
the courage of vulnerability,
the healing of comfort,
the chance for forgiveness and
the touch of a loved hand.

In short, I give you this various earth
for your plaything,
for your life's working
and for your loving...

I doubt there's a better place for it.

Born in Jiangmen

From the dazzling miracle
which is the mind of God
out of the body
of our loving and longing
our wanting and waiting

you were born
into our lives
blessing us
beguiling us with
gladsome sounds
showering winsome smiles

extending our world
and our place in it
beyond old possibilities.

And we for our part
in gratitude will sing to you
laugh with you

teach you what we know of
the beautiful and the difficult
learn from you eagerly
now and when in time
you outstrip us.

We shall weep
when you weep

rejoice in
your rejoicing
and pray for you
earnestly
sometimes desperately

for there is no end
to caring
there are no bounds
to loving.

Forever is too short a time
for the telling of the
whole story.

Lifespan

for L. S.

The sweet spring erupting from
the dark womb of the mountainside
gathering first in a quiet pool of new reflection

spills over its rim, downhill
in a sudden torrent of headlong adolescence

tumbling over the rocks of its bed
in a frenzy of white water

till it reaches the long slow flow
of its deep life's usable river
in the carved valley of its
own persistent making,

at last spreading widely in
the shallow delta of letting go,
loosing its load of accumulated
silt and sediment before merging
gracefully and without regret

with the salt of an infinite sea.

Thundering Surf

In my grandmother's
perverse mind
the thundering surf-sound
is coal delivered
down a metal chute

A Separate Place

For a moment, a death
makes everyone else an outsider,
a foreigner in your separated space.

These foreigners come to you
speaking a different tongue,
carefully translating their words
into flowers and casseroles.

They come bringing with them
the currency of their country,
useless in yours unless
exchanged for your new-minted coin.

They come conscious of being
travelers and trespassers
reading their *Guides Bleus*,
unsure, hesitant, repeating slowly
the useful phrases from
the Book Of Common Words.

The Recently Dead

The recently dead flutter and hover,
unaccustomed to their new transparency.

They're disconcerted by the grieving
in the wake of their awakening,

by the quiet sound of hearts breaking,
of lives falling apart, like glaciers

calving into the deep drowning waters
of the underworld of whales.

They've newly struggled out of
the chrysalis of dying, still uncertain,

do not feel the jagged edge of loss,
are baffled by the freshets of our weeping.

How may we comfort them, untangle
their bewilderment, make them glad?

What Remains

"Even today
at age of seventy-three
I remember the ships' names
as if they were poems"

said the Japanese pilot
trained for the strike.

Arizona   Utah   Nevada

sing the remembered names
for the remembered dead.

Hem of the Past

Only by touching
the hem of the past
can I be made whole.

The Quilt

Within the compass of the quilt
past prints and calicoes carry
their effective histories
into the present.

Unaware, I shift under the
quilted weight of
unremembered things

imagining free will.

Lemon

Bitter yellow lemon, how did you
become companion to sweet
blossoming lily and
candied lemon drop?

How does it happen that
sweet remembering is
companion to old grief?

The gods are jealous of happiness.

The tall man in the sun-bleached overalls
on this cool fair day after rain
knows this when he slides his back
down the willow trunk
to a sitting position in the dappled shade
of the brook-side tree to watch
the glint of day's-end light
play on the wind-ruffled water.

His sons, good sons — his wife, steady
center of his comfort and laughter —
good ancestors before him on this same land,
their spirits at his elbow keeping him company
along the length of turned furrow.

He knows better than to speak of happiness
or count on it beyond this moment —
which he pockets before the gods
can twitch it from him — laughing.

Sirocco

The dry wind
drove sand
in the face of
our first try
at civilization
swept it
deep under
blasted its
memory
left us to
try again
somewhere else
some fertile
river-land
fair enough
to image a
new testament.

Ararat

Still seeking
the tallness of a tree
on which to alight,
the promised olive

emerging from the
vast turbulent waters
of God's disappointment
slowly, too slowly
receding,

the released bird
of our headlong hope
pierces the air
in its searching flight.

Yet again it returns
exhausted
failing to find footing.

Again we revive it,
tend it,
sing to it of our
yearning for a
long-imagined peace

and with an absurdly
irrational patience
launch it once more

into the blue air,
probing for possibilities.

The rainbow signified
there would be
no more all-cleansing
all-renewing floods

so we shall have
to work piecemeal,
make it on our own,
one dove-delivered
branch at a time.

In a Perfect World

In a perfect world nobody would ever
board the wrong train, get a bad haircut,
or spill red wine on a white tablecloth —
no one would marry the wrong person
or have to have a colonoscopy.

In a perfect world your white shoes
and your elegant white handbag
would be the same color white —
you'd never run out of stamps,
nor have your hollandaise separate.

In a perfect world there would be
no "avocado" dinette sets,
rude salespeople, rainy wedding days
or disappointing vacations —
no wet dogs, no bad poems.

In a perfect world one might hope there
would be no ravenous mosquitoes —
but then what would those perfect,
delicate, red-eyed, gossamer-winged,
dusk-darting dragonflies eat?

Some Days

Some days
everything fits,

everything matches,
everything is

as long or as short
as it's supposed to be —

hair, skirt-length,
time, a poem.

Everything smiles
shines and works,

is on sale, stays open late,
falls butter-side up.

Some days — not.

Not Enough

The boy, his family
cracked and ruined,
his small body seething with anger
like hot soup spilling over,
scalding all within his
circle of reach

was sent to live
with his grandmother
who with the informing wisdom
of loving, invited him
to join her in the backyard

to throw eggs. He and
she too — together —
and not just this one time.

Returning home one day
his grandmother found him
tight-fisted, explosive,
throwing rocks.

"What's going on?" she called out,
setting down her groceries.

"There weren't enough eggs!"

Four O'Clock: a Poetry Reading

I would have read your poems
with other emphases than these.

I'd not have understood the good
of giving all the words
long shadows
like the evening's things.

Will you not let me read your creed
without the jagged joke
you yoke to all you say?

I do not think I like your choice of voice.

TV Women

The faces of the women
are too bright
the smile too quick
the eyes too wide with
a breathless enthusiasm
a driven energy.

They swim with sharks
model clothes indistinguishably
purse their lips and kiss smartly
say *Yes!* to TV contracts
new name, new hair color
and marriage equally.

A subcutaneous sheen of
calculation lends added glow
to what these women
and few men know.

Like skipping stones
they shy themselves
across the lake
of perceived advantage

promising all things
pretending all things
pushing the envelope
that contains their ticket home.

The Form Letter

Just above his barely legible signature
Dunston Pingree McCallister says
he is very truly mine.

I am flattered, since he appears to be
a person of significance, professional
standing and personal stature.

I try to imagine his build — substantial?
his face, square-jawed and solemn.
I try to give him a slight smile

but he is serious about being
very truly mine, and his eyes offer himself
to me very truly.

Something, I sense, he is not revealing —
that he has a wife and three children?
That even with a pretty blonde wife

and three exceptional children
he is frighteningly lonely, and so
offers himself, over his gazillion-times

duplicated signature, very truly
to faceless people he's never met,
hoping they may, or at least one may

fill the emptiness in his life
or if not that, at least the emptiness
in his coffers.

It's Once More Spring

It's once more spring when I shall fail — again
to find the words, or gatherings of words
to write the lyrics for the song spring sings,

to celebrate the first great burst of buds
glad greening on the supple, livening limbs
responding to the weather's antic whims...

Now the bouyant spirit skips instead of plods
and we invent a pantheon of gods
to whom to speak our gratitude — again.

The Same Materials

He has a brass bowl
and sees the full
and empty of it.
It becomes the vessel
from which a song spills out.

She comes upon
the dead red fox cub;
for her it shines
with analogy.

The catbird calls
from the sunlit field;
she thinks to bring
Mahler to implant
a new pattern
in its repertoire.

I have a brass bowl.
My lilac has a catbird.
A red fox pauses
at the rise of my field,
alert, sunlit, silhouetted
against the dark of
the wood's edge,

but no poem comes.

Not a Good Cat Day

It's not a good cat day.
The snow melts to slush.
The ducks on the ice edge
wait to slide into the water
at the cat's approach.
The winter-brown grass is
flattened to a soft mudness.

The cat, fur fluffed against the cold,
walks as if to keep all paws
off the ground at once,
at each step shaking off the
miserable wetness with the
complicated embellishment
of a graceless grace note,

an awkwardness, amounting,
for a cat, to a loss of face.
She crouches to threaten
an unconcerned jay, saucy-blue
against the dirty snow-patches,

but the crouch lacks conviction,
back arched stiffly
to keep her underbelly

off the puddled ground.
The pounce lacks heart.

It's not a good cat day.
The world's a sorry place.
There's no fun in it,
nothing to be taken seriously,
only small uncomfortable
humiliations.

The Back Door Cat

As she squatted down on her haunches
my very small daughter found

her curious eyes almost level with those
of the large black cat who'd appeared

at our back door — not begging
but dignified — presenting himself

as one arriving at a restaurant
expecting his reservation to be honored.

He sat like ancient Egypt's regal cats
straight-backed, imperious, unblinking.

The child, as she met the cat's steady stare
gathered words to match her thought.

"His eyes are thinking about his-self."

Calculation

The cat comes
careful not to make friends
only contacts.

Things Noticed

1

where I live
spring comes tight and guarded

it has millennial reasons
not to trust its vulnerable green
to the first blandishments of May

2

the moon is half

not large enough
to start a sudden romance
with anyone who
comes along

but bright enough
to light
remembered tender things

3

caparisoned for the wedding
of summer to winter
a white heron
white chrysanthemum
and a torrent of
hurricane-hurled
white water

4

the first snow
mixed with the last of the
thistle-down
makes an unseasonably
fine flurry

5

The sun shines
and snow falls
as if doing it
for its own pleasure
and in the spirit
of the season

A Melting Place

The sun shines brilliantly,
the sky cloudless, a blue
intense enough to answer
the white intensity of the snow-fields
shouting their bright defiance
to the agent of their demise —

the last cold cry against
the new sun-warmth of noon
gradually sluicing away
the melting remnant
of the stubbornly reactionary
season, with the inevitability

of the Fall of the Roman Empire —
the fall of all things, their season over,
still clinging mindlessly
to old forms of lost power
but unable to prevent the crocus
from melting a place for itself.

Early Morning Beach on an Outgoing Tide

Seaweed scribes the high watermark.

Below it, the hard wet sand tells the
salient facts of a snail's long day's journey,

of the quick sandpipers'
skittering tag with the wash —
no purpose apparent,

of the bubbled breathing of buried clams,
gulls sleeping on one stilt, and the hard
life of a storm-scarred lobster buoy.

Here, the precise stride of
a sunrise-walker.

Above the high watermark
the sand is tumbled

by children's play —
abandoned medieval ruins and
diligent attempts to reach China
using a yellow plastic spade,

by adult play —
casually buried bottle caps,
cigarette butts and the left-over
litter of love-making.

The wise sea tidies the beach it can reach.

The Town pays Joe Willis $6.50 an hour
to rake clean the rest.

Evening Sky

The gale has torn
the clouds to bits in flight —
pale pink, gray, lavender
and shreds of white.

From some far laundry-line
these tatters fly
sailing eastward
on the evening sky.

Helen's Cows

From the field on the other side
of our stone wall comes
a prolonged insistent mooing.
If it were another season
it might signal a calving
but this is the first day of Fall
so it must be the bewildered
anguish of a cow whose calf
has been taken from her —

her calf whose weight
she'd carried inside her,
whom she'd licked clean at birth,
who's tugged at her full udder,
who could find her anywhere
among the wandering herd
and whom she'd watched
fatten and grow handsome.

Helen says when the fattened
vealers are sold for slaughter
their mothers bellow for three
or four days, and then forget.

I want to tell her, "They may quit bawling
but they don't forget...they don't forget. "

Past The Window

From the kitchen-spatter
grease-dust, finger marks
of opening and closing,
of peering and breathing,

past the window
the flash of a bird
unties the eye,

looses it from the
dark place of brooding
to carry it
beyond the pane
to distance

where hills lie at the feet
of mountains and from
ninety-three million miles

the sun
covers them with a
bright blanket of setting.

Topography

I love this rumpled earth,
rocking restless oceans
in its low places,
its casual river-cut valleys

and roundly mounded hills
covered with grazing, planting,
building, singing, mating, weeping

and praying toward
its high places,
the sky-piercing, snow-blessed
mountains where gods walk,
feet untroubled by cold
leaving no footprints.

Foundation

Settled to comfort in a casual chaos,
the great stones of the cellar
of the long-gone barn resemble rubble
but still show evidence of earlier intent
in the cut granite twelve-foot slabs
which a hundred and ninety-six years
of weight-bearing usefulness
have buckled to a new purpose:
the sunning place for ripening grapes.

When the Time is Right

When the time is right
you will walk into the woods
and the trees will speak
each in its own green alphabet.

When the time is right
you will find yourself able to speak
the language of trees sufficiently well
to thank them and ask their forgiveness.

When the time is right
another day, hour, year perhaps
you will come into the company of trees
and there will be no need for speaking.

Tree Lesson

*"Everybody who's anybody longs
to be a tree."* – Rita Dove

The tree does not
think to complain
of its place of growing,

weep for lost
opportunities
or wail over
meaningless mishaps,

envy the luck of
its neighbor
or ponder its
importance in
the Universe,

nor does it
gather guilt in
heavy heaps to
bow its branches
with the cold
load of it.
The spring-sap

runs to new green
and blossoming.

The summer serves
a blithe maturity.

The fall takes
back the green,
replacing it with
wild bedazzlement.

The tree, I think
wastes no regret
on fallen leaves,

is unconcerned
about the question
of what next.

I wish to go to
school to trees.

Where

The rain spits
like a provoked camel
mean-tempered
and resentful.

The wind snarls
in the brush
and whines in
the stand of poplar
at the edge of the marsh

where the heron
has abandoned his
accustomed still vigil —
as has his reflection
in the tidal pool
now wind-shattered.

Where does this serene
long-legged bird go
in harsh and unmerciful
circumstance? Where take
his reflection for safe-keeping?

And I, where do I go?

Winter Solstice

There is cause to be exceeding glad —
to light candles, sing songs, be generous,
eat bountifully of signifying foods,
bring in winter-chilled evergreens
to release their summer-sweet smells
beside the jubilant fire.

Through the intercession of some kindly intelligence,
some good will, some generous disposition,
the chance and fortunate smile of
some beneficent Prime Mover

the days, one by one
are becoming infinitesimally longer,
the gradually-engulfing darkening
which we so feared is reversing itself.

At first we doubted our perception,
we suspected it as illusion —
the desperate child of wishing
but the second day encouraged hope,
the third suggested not a variation but a direction,
on the fourth we joyfully allowed ourselves
to believe we were not to be swallowed up
in darkness totally.

Rejoice and be exceeding glad!
Light returns to us and
there is reason to believe
the earth's slant circling
will bring again the longest day.

Winter Weary

Even the snow is weary
creeping backward from
the road, dreary
with the thrown dirt of plowing,
sunken and diminished

rumpled and pocked
so the tree-shadows
fall wrinkled and inexact
on its tired surface

changed markedly
from the crisply mirrored
lattice of black branches on
the smooth-shining
mid-winter snow-fields.

I too am weary now of winter.
The excitement of it wears thin,
the wonder of it ready
to be packed away with
insulated glove and
fleece-lined boot

for the next new November,
the next season of breathless
anticipation of first snow.

The Steeple Still

The steeple still
signals a village,
though no longer
a traveler's beacon

bespeaking shelter
sustenance, stables and
spiritual certainty.

But still in the valleys
carved from granite
mountains by swift
tumbling rivers

the sky-searching
lightning-rod spire
means you've arrived...

somewhere.

Reclining Mountain

Cloud-shapes lie draped
over the sleeping flanks
of the reclining mountain.

A dark mane of fir and hemlock,
touched at the temples with
white strands of birch, rests
casually on a pillow of snow.

Whether mother, sister,
or lover, you belong to her
and know it, for you are
soothed, cajoled, contented
in her familiar presence.

One day, it is certain,
she will yawn and stretch
and catch your eye

and you will go to her
gladly, as you would climb into
the ample lap of your mother
or lay your head on the
smooth shoulder of your sister,

or lying full length and naked
mount the sun-warmed body
of your lover, as if coming home.

FINALE

The New Face of Old Age

I need now more daisies, fewer orchids
more Wednesdays and fewer Saturdays.
I need larger print, larger sizes
and much larger ice cream cones.

I need shorter lists and longer vacations
more Whitman, less Wordsworth
needles with larger eyes, and
windows with larger views.

I need more Chinese red, less Paynes gray
more reels, fewer dirges
more silliness and banter
less humorless fervor

more puddles, more stars
more old photographs, letters, and shoes
less hurrying, less regret
more attentiveness and noticing.

I need more gentle adequacy
less rigid perfection.
I need more truth-telling fairy tales
and fewer arcane philosophies.

My needs match the slowing of my step
the quickening of my heart
the letting go, the holding fast, and
the unexpected welcoming of change.

NOTES

Dedication: *animae dividium meae* is from Ode 1.3 by Horace, translated by David Ferry as "the other half of my heart."

Page 8: *vademecum*, literally, "go with me," something carried with a person for constant use or reference (a handbook or manual).

Page 8: A *carnet de passage* is a document identifying a driver's vehicle when entering a country temporarily, especially by boat.

Pages 26 and 27: Vesta is the Roman goddess of the hearth and home. The Vestals were chosen to serve in her temple, by the Pontifex Maximus, from among a group of girls 6 to 10 years old, using the priestly formulaic language: *Te, Amata, Capio* ("I take or choose thee, loved one"). These young girls were required to serve for 30 years, their chief duty being to keep the sacred fire burning in the Temple. There were dire and sometimes lethal punishments for allowing the flame to go out.

Page 40: *Lares* and *Penates* were the household gods in Roman times. The *Lares* were the resident ghosts of the dead; the *Penates* lived in the storage cupboards, guardians of the family larder. The rituals connected with them were private and familial.

ABOUT THE AUTHOR

Carol Armstrong has written poetry most of her life, as did her mother before her, on the backs of envelopes and the bottom of grocery lists, usually at 3:00 a.m. when the house was quiet. She went to a small school in Rowayton, Connecticut, where the reading and writing of poetry was not considered either odd or esoteric. So she wrote poetry. She attended Smith College, raised three children (or perhaps, she suggests, they raised her), and shared the career of her husband, who, when he retired as President of Middlebury College, maintained he did so in part to allow her more time for her own creative work, which involved both writing and graphic design. She lives with her husband in Hanover, New Hampshire, though much of her poetry is rooted in their "farm" in Maine.

This book is set in Palatino. Named after Sixteenth Century Italian master of calligraphy Giambattista Palatino, Palatino is based on the humanist fonts of the Italian Renaissance that mirror letters formed by a broad nib pen, giving the typeface a calligraphic grace. But whereas the Renaissance fonts tended to use smaller letters with longer vertical lines and lighter strokes, Palatino is generously proportioned, and is considered to be a much more readable typeface.

To order additional copies of this book
or other Antrim House titles, contact the publisher at

Antrim House
21 Goodrich Rd., Simsbury, CT 06070
860.217.0023, AntrimHouse@comcast.net
or the house website (www.AntrimHouseBooks.com).

•

On the house website
in addition to information on books
you will find sample poems, upcoming events,
and a "seminar room" featuring supplemental biography,
notes, images, poems, reviews, and
writing suggestions.